The Epistles of Peter
Practical Advice for the Last Days

This is a self-study course designed to help you discover for yourself, from the Bible, some important basic truths about the epistles of Peter.

how to study the lesson

1. Try to find a quiet spot free from distractions and noise.

2. Read each question carefully.

3. Look up the Scripture reference given after each question. Make sure you have found the correct Scripture passage. For example, sometimes you will find yourself looking up JOHN 1:1 instead of I JOHN 1:1.

4. Answer the question from the appropriate Bible passage. Write, in your own words, a phrase or sentence to answer the question. In questions that can be answered with a "yes" or "no" always give the reason for your answer . . . "Yes, because. . . ."

5. If possible, keep a dictionary handy in order to look up words you don't understand.

6. Pray for God's help. You *need* God's help in order to understand what you study in the Bible. PSALM 119:18 would be an appropriate verse for you to take to God in prayer.

7. *Class teachers using this course for group study will find some helpful suggestions on page 47.*

how to
take the self-check tests

Each lesson is concluded with a test designed to help you evaluate what you have learned.

1. Review the lesson carefully in the light of the self-check test questions.

2. If there are any questions in the self-check test you cannot answer, perhaps you have written into your lesson the wrong answer from your Bible. Go over your work carefully to make sure you have filled in the blanks correctly.

3. When you think you are ready to take the self-check test, do so without looking up the answers.

4. Check your answers to the self-check test carefully with the answer key given on page 48.

5. If you have any questions wrong, your answer key will tell you where to find the correct answer in your lesson. Go back and locate the right answers. Learn by your mistakes!

apply
what you have learned
to your own life

In this connection, read carefully JAMES 1:22-25. It is only as you apply your lessons to your own life that you will really grow in grace and increase in the knowledge of God.

 Lesson 1

Introduction — The Life of Peter

1 Peter 3:15

Before studying the epistles of Peter, it is important to know something of Peter's life. Our Lord had to mold the life of Peter before Peter could help mold the lives of others. As you study this lesson, look for the ways God works in the lives of His disciples. Then as you study the epistles of Peter, notice how well Peter had learned his lessons from the school of God.

The call of Peter

1. What was Peter's hometown?

JOHN 1:44 _Bethsaida_

The name of this town means "fish town."

2. What was his father's name?

JOHN 1:42; compare MATTHEW 16:17 _Simon son of John   Simon son of Jonah_

3. Who brought Simon to Jesus?

JOHN 1:40; compare 1:42 _Andrew — (Peter's brother)_

4. Give Peter's full name.

II PETER 1:1 _Simon Peter_

5. What new name did Christ give Peter?

JOHN 1:42 _Cephas_

6. What is the meaning of this name?

JOHN 1:42 _translated — Peter_

The word *cephas* is Aramaic, while the Greek synonym is *petros* from which comes the name *Peter*.

Philip   Peter's
Andrew   Brothers

The confession of Peter

Although Christ had changed Simon's name to Peter at his call, the significance of this name did not appear until later.

7. Whom did Peter confess Jesus to be?

MATTHEW 16:16 *You are Christ, the Son of the living God.*

8. Whom did Christ say Peter was?

MATTHEW 16:18 *That he was Peter — the rock — I will build my church.*

This means "stone" or "a piece of rock."

9. Upon what was Christ to build His Church?

MATTHEW 16:18 *the rock.*

10. Who alone is the Rock Foundation of the Church?

I CORINTHIANS 3:11; 10:4; I PETER 2:4; ACTS 4:10, 11 *Jesus Christ — Jesus Christ — Living Stone — Jesus Christ of Nazareth.*

11. Who shared with Jesus in the foundation work of the Church?

EPHESIANS 2:19, 20 *Apostles & prophets.*

12. Did Peter gather from this that Jesus had appointed him to be the foundation of the Church and the first pope? Support your answer. *The stone is living (in that it is personal.)*

I PETER 2:3-7 *like living stones & the Rock.*

13. When Peter had come to see that he was a stone, that is, one with the Rock, what did he call all true believers?

I PETER 2:5; compare EPHESIANS 2:21, 22 _____

The literal translation of "lively" (I PETER 2:5) is "living."

The denial of Peter

Peter experienced spiritual defeats as well as victories. This was the man God chose to write of suffering and subjection. He had learned lessons the hard way so that later he could pass on meaningful instruction.

14. What prediction did Christ make concerning the faithfulness of His disciples?

MARK 14:27 _____

The word "offend" means "to fall" or "to stumble."

15. Give the special prediction of Christ concerning Peter.

MARK 14:30 _____

16. In the midst of such a trial, what was Peter to do?

MARK 14:38 _____

17. What did Peter do instead?

MARK 14:40 _____

18. When the cock crowed twice, how many times had Peter denied he ever knew the Lord?

MARK 14:66-72 _____

19. How did Peter's sin affect him?

MARK 14:72 _____

20. What is the Christian who has sinned always to do?

I JOHN 1:9 _____

The ministry of Peter

Although we often think of the book of Acts as recording the ministry of the apostle Paul, it contains the post-cross ministry of Peter as well. Peter, tempered by the hand and disciplines of God, was used mightily in the opening years of the early Church.

21. Who preached the sermon on the Day of Pentecost?

Acts 2:14 _____

22. What was his message?

Acts 2:36 _____

23. What were the results?

Acts 2:41 _____

24. Describe some of the suffering of Peter.

Acts 5:18; 12:6 _____

25. What was the testimony of ungodly men concerning the witness of Peter in Jerusalem?

Acts 5:28 _____

26. What Christian Jew was the first to give the gospel to the Gentiles?

Acts 10:34; compare 15:7 _____

27. What was the commission to Peter given by our risen Lord (the final mention of Peter in the Gospels)?

John 21:17 _____

28. What charge did Peter later give to his own fellow workers?

I Peter 5:2 _____

The epistles of Peter

Peter had been receiving the news of the persecution of churches everywhere as well as the assault of false teachers upon them. The very name of "Christian" was being exposed to outrage. In his old age, the apostle took up his pen to send forth words of comfort and counsel. In these letters he shows a heart as warm as when he was young, combined with a deeper self-knowledge and humility.

These letters, written A.D. 60 and 66, are a result of the Lord's command to Peter: "Strengthen thy brethren." No letters in the Sacred Canon come more directly home to those in trial and persecution, and those beset with subtle errors are alerted.

check-up time No. 1

You have just studied some important truths about the life of Peter. Review your study by rereading the questions and your written answers. If you aren't sure of an answer, reread the Scripture portion given to see if you can find the answer. Then take this test to see how well you understand important truths you have studied.

In the right-hand margin write "True" or "False" after each of the following statements.

1. Nathanael was the one that brought Peter to Jesus. _F_ 3

2. Peter's name was changed to Cephas by his father. _F_ 5

3. Peter recognized Jesus as the Christ, the Son of the living God. _T_ 7

4. Peter is the rock on which the Church is built. _F_ 10

5. Peter was asked to pray that Christ might not enter into temptation. _F_ 16

6. The Christian who has sinned is always to confess his sin to God. _T_ 20

7. It was Peter who preached on the Day of Pentecost. _T_ 21

8. Although Peter had great blessing, he endured great suffering. _T_ 24

9. Even ungodly men testified to Peter's influence on Jerusalem. _T_ 25

10. Christ told Peter to feed the sheep of God. _T_ 27

Turn to page 48 and check your answers.

 LESSON 2

The Salvation of the Christian

Outline of I Peter
1. The Salvation of the Christian 1:1-25
2. The Subjection of the Christian 2:1—3:12
3. The Suffering of the Christian 3:13—4:19
4. The Service of the Christian 5:1-14

I PETER 1:1-25

The reality of salvation 1:1-12

1. How does Peter represent his authority?

1:1 _____

"The strangers" is literally "the elect sojourners of the dispersion," that is, the Jewish Christians of these particular regions.

2. To whom was Peter called to minister?

GALATIANS 2:7 _____

3. What word indicates that Peter's first epistle is intended primarily for those truly born of the Spirit?

1:2 _____

The word translated "foreknowledge" does not mean "to know beforehand" as the English might convey. It refers to what God would do for men, not what men would do for God. Our election is based on His omniscience and choice because of love (compare ROMANS 8:28-30; ACTS 2:23; I PETER 1:20).

4. What is the essential basis of a believer's sanctification or setting apart unto God?

HEBREWS 10:10 _____

5. Who makes this separation unto God a reality?

1:2 _____

The word "sprinkling" is used in contrast to when Moses sprinkled Israel with the blood of the covenant (EXODUS 24:8). By Israel's contact with the blood, the people were brought within the covenant of which Moses was the mediator (GALATIANS 3:19). Here Peter sees believers brought within the new covenant by the mystical sprinkling of the blood of Christ.

6. Unto what are we begotten?

1:3 _____

The word "lively" means "that which moves in the mind, sparkling, dynamic." It is a favorite word of Peter who delighted to think of life overcoming death through the risen Lord. Christ's resurrection guarantees everything to the believer.

7. Name four characteristics of the believer's inheritance.

1:4 _____

_____

8. While the inheritance is guarded in heaven, what of the believer's personal security while he remains on earth?

1:5 _____

The word here for "kept" is a military term used of those preserved in a fort or a garrisoned town.

9. When is the final display of completed salvation to take place?

1:5; compare I THESSALONIANS 1:10 _____

Underscore the words "through faith." Do not assume that you are one of those kept by Him unless your life is rooted in faith in Christ Jesus.

10. For how long do these testings which bear fruit in rejoicing last?

1:6; compare II CORINTHIANS 4:17 _____

11. What is it that makes for real gold in the character?

JOB 23:10 _____

12. When will we receive the final reward for faithful endurance?

1:7 _____

13. What is the amazing thing about the love people have for Jesus Christ?

1:8; JOHN 20:29 _____

14. Although we do not know Christ after the flesh (II CORINTHIANS 5:16), what feeling may be generated in the heart as a result of spiritual sight?

1:8 _____

15. If we have Him in our hearts by faith, what goal has certainly been attained?

1:9 _____

16. What particular revelations given the prophets concerning Messiah's first coming did they find difficult to understand?

1:11 _____

17. Did Jesus find it difficult to get His own disciples to understand that the cross must precede the crown? Support your answer.

LUKE 24:24-27, 44-46 _____

The prophets of old were also puzzled about the absolute time of His coming and the features that should characterize those times ("what manner of time," I PETER 1:11). As some today try to fix the time of Christ's second coming, so these early prophets tried to settle the precise time He would come.

18. What title does Peter here give the Holy Spirit who was directing the prophets of old to write of the coming redemption?

1:11; compare ROMANS 8:9; GALATIANS 4:6 _____

19. Who, beside those who wrote of these things, were puzzled as to how this salvation would be accomplished?

1:12 _____

The words rendered "look into" mean "to peer deeply into" or "to see to the bottom." Evidently angels learn from us God's plan of salvation.

The results of salvation 1:13-25

20. When will our salvation, the work of divine grace, be consummated?

1:13; compare I THESSALONIANS 1:10 _____

Since such is our hope, we are exhorted to gird up the loins of our minds, thereby presenting a strong front to the adversary at all times.

21. What should be the effect of entertaining such a hope?

1:14 _____

22. What should be our daily goal?

1:15 _____

23. Since we know our Heavenly Father is going to judge and reward us on the basis of our works, how should we conduct ourselves?

1:17 _____

The word translated "fear" means "reverential awe," not terror (compare PROVERBS 1:7).

24. What, after all, should be the strongest incentive to holy living?

1:18, 19 _____

25. Since we are bought with such a price, what is our supreme obligation?

I CORINTHIANS 6:20 _____

26. What, beside the blood of Christ, is incorruptible?

1:23 _____

27. For how long will the Word of the Lord last?

1:25 _____

28. With what, then, should the believer be occupied?

2:2 _____

check-up time No. 2

You have just studied some important truths about the salvation of the Christian. Now take this test to see how well you understand important truths you have studied.

Circle the letter of the correct or most nearly correct answer.

1. The First Epistle of Peter was addressed to (a) the unsaved, (b) Gentile Christians, (c) Jewish Christians.

2. The basis of sanctification is (a) the death of Christ, (b) the indwelling Spirit, (c) the love of God.

3. The Agent of sanctification is (a) the Father, (b) the Son, (c) the Holy Spirit.

4. The believer's inheritance is (a) corruptible, (b) reserved in heaven, (c) defiled.

5. The testing of Christians is (a) temporary, (b) endless, (c) needless.

6. If we have Christ in our hearts by faith, then we are (a) unable to sin, (b) saved, (c) sure to avoid suffering.

7. Concerning Christ's coming, we are to know (a) the facts, not the time, (b) the time, not the facts, (c) neither the time nor the facts.

8. Peter points out that the angels learn about man's redemption from (a) God in heaven, (b) observing wicked men, (c) observing believers.

9. The strongest motive for holy living should be (a) the price Christ paid, (b) the peril we face, (c) the prestige it brings.

10. The believer should be occupied with (a) man's wisdom, (b) God's Word, (c) Satan's wickedness.

Turn to page 48 and check your answers.

 LESSON 3

The Subjection of the Christian

I PETER 2:1—3:12

The basis of subjection 2:1-10

The reason for our conduct in the Christian life is our relationship and position in Christ. We are to *become* what we already *are*. Thus in this section Peter shows that we are living stones and a royal priesthood as the basis for the responsibilities and obligations of our Christian life.

1. When one becomes a Christian, what is he to do with specific sin in his life?

2:1 _____

2. What special appetite should new Christians deliberately cultivate?

2:2 _____

3. Why are some Christians so content with the first principles (milk) of Christian truth?

I CORINTHIANS 3:2, 3 _____

In I PETER 2:4 the imagery changes from the growth of babies to that of a building in which each believer is a living stone.

4. How did the prophet Isaiah refer to the coming Messiah?

ISAIAH 28:16; compare 2:4 _____

5. Who are the "living stones" who comprise the spiritual house, the Church?

2:5; compare Ephesians 2:20-22 _____

It is interesting that many names which belong to Christ in the singular are assigned to Christians in the plural, such as stones, priests, kings, sons, etc.

6. Name the spiritual sacrifices believers offer.

a. Romans 12:1 _____

b. Hebrews 13:15 _____

c. Hebrews 13:16 _____

d. Hebrews 13:16 _____

To "communicate" in the sense the word is used here means to "have fellowship."

7. If one is really united to the Chief Corner Stone by the Holy Spirit, what should be the effect?

2:6 _____

"Confounded" is literally "put to shame."

8. Who alone can discern the preciousness of Christ?

2:7 _____

9. To whom is He a stone of stumbling and rock of offense?

2:8; compare II Corinthians 2:15, 16 _____

10. Give the titles for believers in verse 9.

2:9 _____

11. What are they called in verse 11?

2:11 _____

12. Through every phase of the Christian life, what is our main object?

2:9 _____

13. How as a "peculiar people" should we distinguish ourselves?

TITUS 2:14 _____

The phrase translated "peculiar people" really signifies "a people for a possession." In common usage the word *peculiar* has come to mean odd. However the thought of the original is that as a purchased people we should seek to glorify God (I CORINTHIANS 6:19, 20).

Subjection to the state 2:11-17

14. As those who are journeying home through a godless world, against what should we especially be guarded?

2:11 _____

15. What should be the constant answer of our lives to the world's ridicule?

2:12; compare ROMANS 12:17 _____

16. Why should the Christian be law-abiding under any form of government?

2:13; compare ROMANS 13:1-7 _____

17. How are we to stop the mouths of foolish men?

2:15 _____

Subjection in the household 2:18-25

18. How were those who worked for hard taskmasters to witness for Christ?

2:18 _____

19. Who is to be considered the workers' real Employer?

EPHESIANS 6:5-7 _____

20. Despite ill treatment received from an unjust employer, what is the comfort of the one who serves as unto Christ?

EPHESIANS 6:8; compare COLOSSIANS 3:22-25 _____

21. If one, in his consciousness of God, quietly endures hard conditions, who will see that he is justly paid?

2:19 _____

The word rendered "thankworthy" is commonly rendered "grace." In LUKE 6:32 ("What *thank* have ye?") the context shows it is equivalent to a reward. Likewise here it also means a reward from God.

22. What is one sure way to lay up eternal reward?

2:20 _____

23. How are we to regard "personal rights" if we are walking in the steps of Christ (2:21)?

2:22, 23 _____

24. Besides being an example, what other significance did the sufferings of Jesus have?

2:24; compare ISAIAH 53:5, 6 _____

25. "What does the risen Christ become to those who are saved through Him?

2:25 _____

Subjection in the family 3:1-12

26. What reason is given as to why Christian wives should be quietly submissive, especially when their husbands are unbelievers?

3:1, 2 _____

The word "subjection" has no thought of inferiority or servile subjection. It describes the relation peculiar to believers, that is, the Christian grace of yielding one's preferences to another. The phrase "without the word" is literally "without speech," meaning the silent preaching of conduct.

27. Are makeup and jewelry the best kind of adornment for women to wear?

3:3 _____

28. What is to shine forth as the true character of the Christian woman?

3:4 _____

29. Who is cited from Old Testament times as a wife who was properly subject to her husband?

3:6 _____

The last phrase of verse 6, "not afraid with any amazement," is better rendered, "not terrorized by any fear." The idea is that Christian wives were not expected to tremble from the angry threats of unbelieving husbands. Knowing that she was doing the will of God, the believing wife should go about her duties with cheerful tranquility.

30. What consideration is a Christian husband expected to show toward his wife?

3:7 _____

31. When such consideration is lacking, what is often the result?

3:7 _____

32. For what special qualities does Peter plead?

3:8 _____

The word rendered "pitiful" means "tenderhearted" or "compassionate."

33. What does a Christian forfeit when he resorts to vindictiveness in any form?

3:9 _____

34. Who properly handles all matters of rendering punishment in cases of personal affront?

Romans 12:19 _____

35. What is one way to prolong life with good days?

3:10 _____

36. Of what two facts should we constantly remind ourselves?

3:12 _____

check-up time No. 3

You have just studied some important truths about the subjection of the Christian. Review your study by rereading the questions and your written answers. If you aren't sure of an answer, reread the Scripture portion given to see if you can find the answer. Then take this test to see how well you understand important truths you have studied.

In the right-hand margin write "True" or "False" after each of the following statements.

1. The believer should deliberately cultivate an appetite for God's Word. _____

2. Peter declares that believers are to offer spiritual sacrifices to God. _____

3. Peter admonishes believers to be "peculiar" in the sense of being "odd." _____

4. Believers are to do good as a testimony to the unsaved. _____

5. The real Employer of Christian employees is Christ Himself. _____

6. Peter shows that God will reward us if we suffer for our faults. _____

7. Believers can suffer in every way Christ did. _____

8. Peter says that the wife is inferior to the husband. _____

9. Unbelieving husbands may be won to Christ through the way their Christian wives conduct themselves. _____

10. Peter relieves husbands of responsibility toward their wives. _____

Turn to page 48 and check your answers.

 LESSON 4

The Suffering of the Christian

I PETER 3:13—4:19

The suffering of the Christian is God's means of applying the Christian life and preparing us for effective service. In this section, Peter shows the suffering of the Christian as both citizen and saint.

Suffering as a citizen 3:13—4:6

1. How does Peter describe those who suffer for righteousness' sake?

3:14 _____

2. When people would know the reason for our hope and peace, with what should we be ready?

3:15 _____

3. How is this answer to be given?

3:15 _____

4. What will happen to those evildoers who falsely accuse our good Christian behavior?

3:16 _____

5. When Peter is speaking of suffering righteously, who comes to his mind?

3:18 _____

21

6. What is the difference between Christ's sufferings at the hands of men and any suffering we may be called upon to endure?

3:18 _____

7. After His death, to whom did Christ proclaim a message?

3:19; compare Hebrews 1:13, 14 _____

Many hold that verses 19, 20 refer to Christ's judicial proclamation of His victory on the cross to wicked confined angels (compare II Peter 2:4; Jude 6). Some of the reasons for this are that the order of the passage shows that this was after Christ's death; the word "spirits" (v. 19) often refers to angels (Hebrews 1:7, 14); the word "preached" (v. 19) means "to proclaim a message," not necessarily the gospel; and verse 20 refers to specific sin during the time of Noah (compare Genesis 6:2; II Peter 2:4; Jude 6). The point is that Genesis 3:15 gives the promise of Messiah's victory over Satan and his forces. However Satan attempted to corrupt the line of woman (Genesis 6:2), but after the fulfillment of Genesis 3:15 (John 12:31; 16:11; Colossians 2:14, 15), Christ proclaimed His victory to those involved in this corrupt and sinful plan.

8. Is water baptism a washing of the soul from the defilement of sin ("the filth of the flesh")? Support your answer.

3:21 _____

9. What is one important function of baptism?

3:21, 22; compare Romans 6:4, 5 _____

Baptism signifies the answer of a good conscience, that is, the consciousness of not having a debt standing against the soul. Water saved Noah, not of itself, but by sustaining the ark built on faith, resting on God's Word. It was to Noah a sign of the coming regeneration of the earth. So water baptism "saves"—not of itself, but through the spiritual reality connected with it—faith in Christ crucified, buried, risen—of which baptism is a sign and seal.

10. What is almost sure to be a part of the experience of a true Christian?

4:1 _____

The apostle John vigorously presses the truth that the Son of God was *manifested* in the flesh. Peter, on the other hand, presses the point that He had *suffered* in the flesh, and that all who truly follow Him should expect to suffer in some degree, finding in Him grace to endure unto the end.

11. How does suffering for Christ affect our conduct?

4:1, 2; compare ROMANS 6:7-11 _____

In the earnestness of the Christian life lies a large degree of safety from surrounding evils.

12. When one learns the blessedness of suffering in God's will, what effect does it have on the old self-will?

4:2 _____

13. For what does one lose his appetite when Christ becomes supreme in his heart?

4:3 _____

14. Why do Christians not need to be disturbed by the mockings of the unsaved?

4:5 _____

In verse 6, Peter is referring to the gospel being preached to Christians before they died. They had the judgment of men while they were alive, but will live again and enjoy eternal life with God (compare verse 13).

Suffering as a saint 4:7-19

15. Of what great event did Peter have a vivid realization?

4:7 _____

16. What is all-essential for those who profess the name of Christ?

4:8 _____

This is literally "stretched-out love," a love that never tires.

17. Instead of delighting in undue disclosings of the failings of others, what does such love do?

4:8; compare I CORINTHIANS 13:5-7 _____

18. What does the Holy Spirit seek to utilize for the glory of Christ?

4:10; compare ROMANS 12:6-8; I CORINTHIANS 7:7 _____

19. In what manner are we to speak for Christ?

4:11 _____

20. What is to be our goal in the use of all our gifts?

4:11; compare I CORINTHIANS 10:31 _____

21. What purpose is served by the fiery trials of Christians?

4:12; compare 1:7 _____

22. If we are mindful of God's Word, what will be our reaction to severe testings?

4:13 _____

23. What kind of trial is harder to bear than bodily suffering or difficult circumstances?

4:14 _____

24. If this kind of reproach is bravely endured, what blessed assurance does it bring?

4:14 _____

25. Can one witness effectively for Christ by the very way in which he suffers injustice? Give a reason for your answer.

4:16 _____

26. What was Peter expecting to come upon the churches shortly?

4:17 _____

27. What effect did he feel this time of judgment would have on many church members?

4:18 _____

28. As for those who were being called to endure many trials for Jesus' sake, what sole concern did they need to have?

4:19 _____

check-up time No. 4

You have just studied some important truths about the suffering of the Christian. Now take this test to see how well you understand important truths you have studied.

Circle the letter of the correct or most nearly correct answer.

1. When people want to know the reason for the peace in our hearts, we should give them (a) an argument, (b) an apology, (c) an answer.

2. Evildoers who falsely accuse us will be (a) ashamed, (b) imprisoned, (c) persecuted.

3. The Christian's supreme example in suffering is (a) Peter, (b) Christ, (c) Paul.

4. Peter shows that baptism (a) removes sin, (b) brings about salvation, (c) illustrates salvation.

5. Suffering according to the will of God makes our interest in sin (a) increase, (b) decrease, (c) stay the same.

6. Peter constantly kept in mind (a) the end of all things, (b) the course of current events, (c) the origins of the universe.

7. The greatest virtue Peter exhorts us to have is (a) patience, (b) joy, (c) love.

8. Our God-given abilities should be used to (a) glorify God, (b) glorify ourselves, (c) compete with others.

9. The purpose of the Christian's fiery trials is to (a) punish him, (b) try him, (c) discourage him.

10. When a Christian suffers for Christ's sake he should (a) complain, (b) tell everybody about it, (c) rejoice.

Turn to page 48 and check your answers.

 LESSON 5

The Service of the Christian

I PETER 5:1-14

In this last section of the first letter, the apostle instructs believers concerning their Christian service. He gives injunctions to members of the church, dealing with the way they should occupy their respective positions and bear themselves toward each other. He also gives injunctions to aid believers in their spiritual warfare.

Service in the church 5:1-7

1. Instead of laying claim to primacy, how does Peter refer to his relationship to the churches?

5:1 _____

2. On what occasion was Peter "a partaker of the glory that shall be revealed"?

5:1; MATTHEW 17:1-8 _____

3. How does Peter describe his relationship to the sufferings of Christ?

5:1 _____

4. What does he define as the first duty of elders?

5:2 _____

The word rendered "feed" has the broader meaning of "tend."

5. What in Peter's own experience probably prompted this counsel?

JOHN 21:15-17 _____

6. What similar counsel do we have from Paul?

ACTS 20:28 _____

7. In what spirit is this feeding or tending to be discharged?

5:2 _____

The word "lucre," used five times in the New Testament and meaning "ill-gotten gain," is in every case directed to Christian workers, not merchants. Even in the troubled times of Peter's day, there was apparently money here and there to influence elders in various ways.

8. What characteristic of scribes and Pharisees had Jesus so strongly denounced?

MATTHEW 23:14 _____

9. What is one of the proper characteristics of a deacon?

I TIMOTHY 3:8 _____

10. Why do some Christian workers teach views that are tolerant of sin?

TITUS 1:11 _____

11. What is always the proper attitude of an elder?

5:3; compare I TIMOTHY 4:12 _____

The word "heritage" is the Greek word *kleros* from which comes "clergy." The minister is no more "clergy" than others of the flock. He is not a person set on a pedestal, but a fellow servant with a special calling to guard and teach the flock of God.

12. As Peter here addresses shepherds of the flock, what title, nowhere else given, does he bestow upon Christ?

5:4; compare JOHN 10:11; HEBREWS 13:20 _____

13. With what aspect of Christ's program is it connected?

5:4 _____

14. Give the remedy for most of the difficulties that arise in churches.

5:5 _____

15. What human characteristic does God single out as one of the great hindrances to His work?

5:5 _____

16. Who is it that will exalt the truly humble?

5:6 _____

17. What is our responsibility if we expect God to care for us?

5:7 _____

One translation is "casting all your business in to him." One who is humble-minded toward God will not try to keep his own cares, but will commit all to the Father, being sure of His concern.

Service as a Christian 5:8-14

18. What special reason did Peter have for believing in a personal devil (5:8)?

LUKE 22:31, 32 _____

19. To what does he compare this adversary?

5:8 _____

20. Give the names of other deadly creatures that Satan is called.

REVELATION 20:2 _____

21. What stronger Lion does the believer have on his side?

REVELATION 5:5 _____

22. Over against the "adversary," what does the Christian have?

I JOHN 2:1 _____

23. How only can a spiritual adversary be faced?

5:9 _____

24. What is "above all" in our spiritual equipment?

EPHESIANS 6:16 _____

25. What results from the believer's patient endurance?

5:10 _____

One translation of "make you perfect" is "mend you," and the word rendered "strengthen" means "give you power to resist attack." Certainly this is a power we often need.

26. For whom only is there real peace under all circumstances?

5:14 _____

check-up time No. 5

You have just studied some important truths about the service of the Christian. Review your study by rereading the questions and your written answers. If you aren't sure of an answer, reread the Scripture portion given to see if you can find the answer. Then take this test to see how well you understand important truths you have studied.

In the right-hand margin write "True" or "False" after each of the following statements.

1. Peter was an elder in the early church. _____

2. Elders are to feed the flock of God willingly. _____

3. The teaching of elders is to be influenced by the money they receive. _____

4. Ministers are to be examples to the flock of God. _____

5. Peter points out that in the house of God subjection is to be disregarded. _____

6. The truly humble will be exalted in due time. _____

7. The believer need have no cares to burden him. _____

8. Our responsibility is to resist Satan. _____

9. Suffering is often remedial and strengthening. _____

10. Peter's closing benediction is one of peace. _____

Turn to page 48 and check your answers.

 LESSON 6

The Assurance of Doctrine

II PETER 1:1-21

II Peter – to stimulate Christian
1. growth;
2. combat false teaching;
3. encourage watchfulness in view

The Second Epistle of Peter was written to fortify believers in the endurance of afflictions and persecutions. It stresses watchfulness against perils from false teachers. The epistle may be outlined as follows: *of the Lord's certain return.*

1. The Assurance of Doctrine 1
2. The Admonition Against Denial 2
3. The Attitude Toward Destiny 3

The first chapter shows the importance of God's Word as to what it teaches Christians and as to its certainty.

The provision for stability 1:1-15

This first section points out that Christians are not only to know the truth of God's Word, but also to be stabilized in it (1:12). The stability of the believer is based on the Word of God.

1. On what condition is the increase of grace and peace given in the life of the believer?

1:2; compare 3:18 _Grow in knowledge_

2. How do we come to possess the things that pertain to life and godliness?

1:3 _____

3. What is the medium through which we become partakers of the divine nature?

1:4; compare ROMANS 1:16; 10:17 _____

4. What accompanies the experience of the new birth?

1:4; compare II CORINTHIANS 5:17 _____

5. What must be added to this newly-implanted nature?

1:5-7 _____

6. What subtractions should one make?

I PETER 2:1 _____

7. What will be the net result of these subtractions and additions?

1:8 _____

8. Against what common trait of the mind must we be constantly on guard?

1:9 _____

9. When one finds his delight in God and in the service of His Son, what can he confidently conclude?

1:10 _____

The insuring of one's election is spoken of, not in respect of God, for there is no uncertainty on His part, but on our part. Real joy comes out of being sure we are saved. That does not come by sitting down and waiting for religious feelings. Active pursuit of spiritual things and the service of Christ is the quickest way to find inner assurance that the Holy Spirit is indwelling.

10. What phase of truth should the Christian teacher emphasize?

1:12; compare 1:4-7 _____

11. How long did Peter intend to keep reiterating the same truths?

1:13 _____

12. What provision was Peter making as he looked to his departure from this life?

1:15 _____

The prophecy that is sure 1:16-21

The apostle now moves from what is found in the Scriptures to the Scriptures themselves.

13. Instead of having to make up a clever fable, how did Peter regard himself?

1:16 _____

14. To what supernatural event from heaven did Peter bear witness?

1:17; compare MATTHEW 17:1-8 _____

15. What do we have that is more sure than any vision?

1:19 _____

16. What is to be the believer's attitude to the Scriptures?

1:19 _____

17. What great dawn does Peter have in mind?

3:3, 4; compare TITUS 2:13 _____

18. Where does the Scripture not originate?

1:20 _____

This verse is not a protest against private judgment in interpreting. One translation is "no prophecy of the Scripture originates from one's own interpretation." The Bible is the divine viewpoint, not the human viewpoint.

19. Did prophets sometimes write things which were entirely beyond their own understanding? Support your answer.

I PETER 1:10-12; compare DANIEL 12:8-10 _____

Difficult Scriptures cannot be interpreted by readers any more than by the writers, by their own private and human powers. Spiritual discernment is needed and imparted by the Holy Spirit, the Author and Supreme Interpreter (JOHN 16:14).

20. Were the prophets of the Bible at any time anything more than instruments? Support your answer.

1:21; compare I CORINTHIANS 2:13 _____

21. How were they moved, that is borne along, by the Holy Spirit to write the prophecies, even though often they could not understand the meaning?

1:21 _____

The Scriptures have their source in God with chosen men acting as instruments superintended by the Holy Spirit. This is the miracle of inspiration, the accurate transcription of God's truth to men. This is why it is a more sure word of prophecy.

check-up time No. 6

You have just studied some important truths about the assurance of doctrine. Now take this test to see how well you understand important truths you have studied.

Circle the letter of the correct or most nearly correct answer.

1. Grace and peace of the believer are increased through (a) the love of God, (b) the knowledge of God, (c) the fear of God.

2. Because the believer has been born again, he has (a) a divine nature, (b) no more temptation, (c) lost his corrupt old nature.

3. Peter says that the believer should add to his faith (a) virtue, knowledge and temperance, (b) patience, godliness, brotherly kindness and charity, (c) all of these.

4. God-given virtues in the life make the believer (a) fruitful, (b) forgetful of his past, (c) fretful about his failings.

5. Peter wanted the believers to remember God's Word so that they would be (a) knowledgeable, (b) established, (c) elected.

6. Peter wanted Christians to be reminded of these things in case he (a) denied the Lord again, (b) was imprisoned, (c) died.

7. Peter points out that he was an eyewitness of Christ's (a) transfiguration, (b) baptism, (c) temptation.

8. The Scriptures are better for us as a means of faith than (a) visions, (b) tongues, (c) both of these.

9. The Scriptures originated with (a) man, (b) the angels, (c) God.

10. The writers of Scripture understood (a) none of what they wrote, (b) some of what they wrote, (c) all of what they wrote.

Turn to page 48 and check your answers.

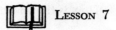

LESSON 7

The Admonition Against Denial

II PETER 2:1-22

The tone of the epistle now changes from grave exhortation to stern warning concerning error. Having set forth the true light, Peter now puts his readers on guard against dangerous false teachers. Woe to all who demoralize the Christian Church through false teaching:

The conduct of false teachers 2:1-3

1. Compare Peter's prediction with that of our Lord.

2:1; compare MATTHEW 24:24 _____

The word "privily" means "to bring in by the side." It has the idea of secrecy, insidiousness, error slyly mixed with truth. The phrase "damnable heresies" is literally "heresies of destruction."

2. How does Paul express the slyness of false teachers?

GALATIANS 2:4 _____

3. What does Jude say of them?

JUDE 4 _____

4. What particular truth do most false teachers seek to eliminate?

2:1; compare 1:18, 19 _____

5. What will greed cause false teachers to do?

2:3 _____

37

6. How is the construction of their speeches described?

2:3; compare ROMANS 16:18 _____

7. Regardless of their sweet spirit and fair words, what is on the way for teachers of error?

2:3 _____

The condemnation of false teachers 2:4-14

In verses 4-6 Peter gives three examples of divine judgment which overtook the enemies of truth.

8. What happened to the angels that sinned?

2:4 _____

The word rendered "hell" is the Greek word *tartarus*. It means "the lowest abyss, a place for gross offenders." This is the only time it is used in the New Testament.

9. Is this the final state of wicked angels? Give a reason for your answer.

2:4; compare JUDE 6 _____

10. What is the second great class of rebels of whom Peter reminds us?

2:5; compare MATTHEW 24:38, 39 _____

11. What is the third illustration of swift judgment?

2:6, 7; compare GENESIS 19 _____

12. What one thing is said to the credit of Lot?

2:7 _____

Lot was sore distressed or worn out with the evil ways of Sodom. The word "vexed" in verse 8 is different from verse 7 and means "tortured" or "tormented."

13. In spite of Lot's worldliness, what is said of his soul and of the man himself?

2:8 _____

14. What is always certain for those who love God?

2:9; compare Job 5:19 _____

15. What is the certain fate of those who reject the truth of God?

2:9 _____

The correct rendering here is "reserve the unrighteous under punishment unto the day of judgment." This suggests that even in this life they sustain a certain measure of punishment which will be consummated later if they are not converted.

16. Upon what class is judgment certainly to descend?

2:10 _____

17. If angels dare not judge and speak evil, what of men who presume to condemn the truth of God?

2:10-12 _____

18. What will be the reward of the teachers of error who make sport of basic truth?

2:13 _____

19. What do some false teachers reveal in their very eyes?

2:14; compare Matthew 5:28; Revelation 2:20-22 _____

20. What kind of people are most easily beguiled by false teaching?

2:14; compare James 1:8; II Timothy 3:6 _____

The character of false teachers 2:15-22

21. Who is mentioned as an example of one who turned spiritual gifts to his own profit?

2:15; compare NUMBERS 22:5-7 _____

22. To what are people compared who have forsaken revealed truth?

2:17; JEREMIAH 2:13 _____

23. Where alone can satisfaction be found for the thirsty soul?

JOHN 4:14 _____

24. Describe the hopeless estate of apostates.

2:17 _____

25. How do false teachers often make their appeal to human nature?

2:18 _____

The expression "clean escaped" should be rendered "those who are just escaping." The idea is that those who are just beginning to think are the ones often taken in by the flesh-pleading bait false teachers have to offer.

26. While false teachers promise freedom from restraints of the gospel, what do they actually do?

2:19 _____

27. What is usually the result of one who turns from the world for a season and then becomes entangled again?

2:20; compare MATTHEW 12:43-45 _____

28. What is better than turning aside from the truth?

2:21 _____

29. As to these particular false teachers, what is Peter's double comparison?

2:22 _____

30. What is a basic characteristic of the unregenerate?

PROVERBS 26:11 _____

31. What is characteristic of a true Christian though he may occasionally fall by the wayside?

PSALM 40:2 _____

The point of Peter's statement is that the nature of the unsaved has never really been changed. They may have reformed temporarily, but they were easily drawn back to the trends of their own natures. Man must be changed on the inside first.

check-up time No. 7

You have just studied some important truths about the admonition against denial. Review your study by rereading the questions and your written answers. If you aren't sure of an answer, reread the Scripture portion given to see if you can find the answer. Then take this test to see how well you understand important truths you have studied.

In the right-hand margin write "True" or "False" after each of the following statements.

1. Peter shows that false teachers in the church are obvious to all. _____

2. The second coming of Christ is the main truth denied by false teachers. _____

3. Peter declares that false teachers will be judged. _____

4. Fallen angels are yet to be judged by God. _____

5. Lot was evidently an unsaved man. _____

6. It is an unquestionable fact that the unjust will be punished. _____

7. The lustful eyes of some false teachers betray them. _____

8. Balaam is an example of a man who misused spiritual gifts for worldly gain. _____

9. False teachers usually deceive those who are just beginning to show an interest in spiritual things. _____

10. Man must be regenerated before he can be permanently reformed. _____

Turn to page 48 and check your answers.

 Lesson 8

The Attitude Toward Destiny

II Peter 3:1-18

This last chapter is a fitting conclusion to both epistles, for it summarizes many of Peter's themes. But more than that, this chapter looks forward to the future hope of every believer in Christ and the life we should live in light of His future coming.

The ignorance of Christ's coming 3:1-7

1. What fact concerning the end days of the age had been clearly impressed on Peter's mind?

3:1-3 _____

2. What is the natural cause of a spirit of cynicism and scoffing?

3:3 _____

3. What particular truth may we expect Satan's followers to dislike?

3:4; compare MATTHEW 24:48-51 _____

4. Is this spirit due to mere lack of instruction? Support your answer.

3:5 _____

5. What form of catastrophe came upon the original world?

3:5, 6 _____

43

6. Describe the next form of judgment to overtake the world.

3:7 _____

The word rendered "perdition" is the same as that translated "destruction" in 2:1 and "perished" in 3:6. Obviously it does not mean annihilation but rather destruction or ruin.

The instruction of Christ's coming 3:8-18

7. What is the answer to the argument that everything has continued without a break for centuries (3:4)?

3:8; compare PSALM 90:4 _____

8. Since God is not slack concerning His promise, why has He delayed for such a long time?

3:9 _____

9. What is God's great desire?

I TIMOTHY 2:4; compare EZEKIEL 18:23 _____

10. Describe the way the Day of the Lord will come.

3:10 _____

_____

The Day of the Lord is not concerned with the blessing of the saints, but rather with the aspect of judgment at the end of the age (JOEL 1:15; ISAIAH 2:12-19; EZEKIEL 13:5; MALACHI 3:2).

11. What will be the climax of these earth judgments of end time?

3:10 _____

12. Besides this earth, what else is to be affected?

3:10 _____

13. What will result from the scorching heat?

3:10 _____

14. What in particular will be consumed?

3:10 _____

15. Knowing that the very fabric of man's order of things is to be completely wiped out, what question is posed for every serious thinker?

3:11 _____

16. What will God create immediately after purging this earth?

3:13; compare Isaiah 65:17 _____

17. How should the knowledge that our Lord is to establish an entirely new order affect all true believers?

3:14 _____

18. What does Peter say about the epistles of Paul?

3:15, 16 _____

_____

19. What is Peter's final warning?

3:17 _____

20. Give Peter's final exhortation.

3:18 _____

21. Along what two lines must we ever seek to grow?

3:18 _____

One who grows in grace without knowledge of the Word becomes a "hothouse" Christian. To grow in knowledge without accompanying grace is to be equally ineffective. We must have the Word as food for the soul, study it regularly and systematically, and always be fully yielded to the Spirit's control.

check-up time No. 8

You have just studied some important truths about the attitude toward destiny. Now take this test to see how well you understand important truths you have studied.

Circle the letter of the correct or most nearly correct answer.

1. Peter said that in the last days would come (a) Satan, (b) Judas, (c) scoffers.

2. Satan's followers especially dislike the Bible's teaching about (a) the coming of Christ, (b) the Flood, (c) inspiration.

3. Peter condemns these people because they are willingly (a) rebellious, (b) ignorant, (c) disbelieving.

4. The reason that God has delayed His coming for so long is because He is (a) holy, (b) just, (c) longsuffering.

5. The desire of God is for (a) all to be saved, (b) some to be saved, (c) some to be punished.

6. Peter declares that God will destroy (a) this earth, (b) the heavens, (c) the heavens and the earth.

7. The believer is to live in light of the destruction of (a) God's order, (b) man's order, (c) God's Word.

8. After God purges the earth, He will make (a) a new people, (b) a new heaven and earth, (c) new angels.

9. Peter's final warning was about (a) instability, (b) inactivity, (c) infidelity.

10. Peter's final exhortation is to (a) grow in grace, (b) pray earnestly, (c) give cheerfully.

Turn to page 48 and check your answers.

Suggestions for class use

1. The class teacher may wish to tear this page from each workbook as the answer key is on the reverse side.

2. The teacher should study the lesson first, filling in the blanks in the workbook. He should be prepared to give help to the class on some of the harder places in the lesson. He should also take the self-check tests himself, check his answers with the answer key and look up any question answered incorrectly.

3. Class sessions can be supplemented by the teacher's giving a talk or leading a discussion on the subject to be studied. The class could then fill in the workbook together as a group, in teams, or individually. If so desired by the teacher, however, this could be done at home. The self-check tests can be done as homework by the class.

4. The self-check tests can be corrected at the beginning of each class session. A brief discussion of the answers can serve as review for the previous lesson.

5. The teacher should motivate and encourage his students. Some public recognition might well be given to class members who successfully complete this course.

answer key
to self-check tests

Be sure to look up any questions you answered incorrectly.

Q gives the number of the test question.

A gives the correct *answer*.

R *refers* you back to the number of the question in the lesson itself, where the correct answer is to be found.

Mark with an "x" your wrong answers.

TEST 1			TEST 2			TEST 3			TEST 4		
Q	A	R	Q	A	R	Q	A	R	Q	A	R
1	F	3	1	c	1	1	T	2	1	c	2
2	F	5	2	a	4	2	T	6	2	a	4
3	T	7	3	c	5	3	F	13	3	b	5
4	F	10	4	b	7	4	T	15	4	c	9
5	F	16	5	a	10	5	T	19	5	b	11
6	T	20	6	b	15	6	F	22	6	a	15
7	T	21	7	a	17	7	T	24	7	c	16
8	T	24	8	c	19	8	F	26	8	a	20
9	T	25	9	a	24	9	T	26	9	b	21
10	T	27	10	b	28	10	F	30	10	c	24

TEST 5			TEST 6			TEST 7			TEST 8		
Q	A	R	Q	A	R	Q	A	R	Q	A	R
1	T	1	1	b	1	1	F	1	1	c	2
2	T	4	2	a	4	2	F	4	2	a	3
3	F	7	3	c	5	3	T	7	3	b	4
4	T	11	4	a	7	4	T	9	4	c	8
5	F	14	5	b	10	5	F	13	5	a	9
6	T	16	6	c	12	6	T	15	6	c	10
7	T	17	7	a	14	7	T	19	7	b	15
8	T	23	8	c	15	8	T	21	8	b	16
9	T	25	9	c	18	9	T	25	9	c	19
10	T	26	10	b	19	10	T	31	10	a	21

how well did you do?

0-1 wrong answers—excellent work

2-3 wrong answers—review errors carefully

4 or more wrong answers—restudy the lesson before going on to the next one